LEGENDARY LIVES

Fred Rogers

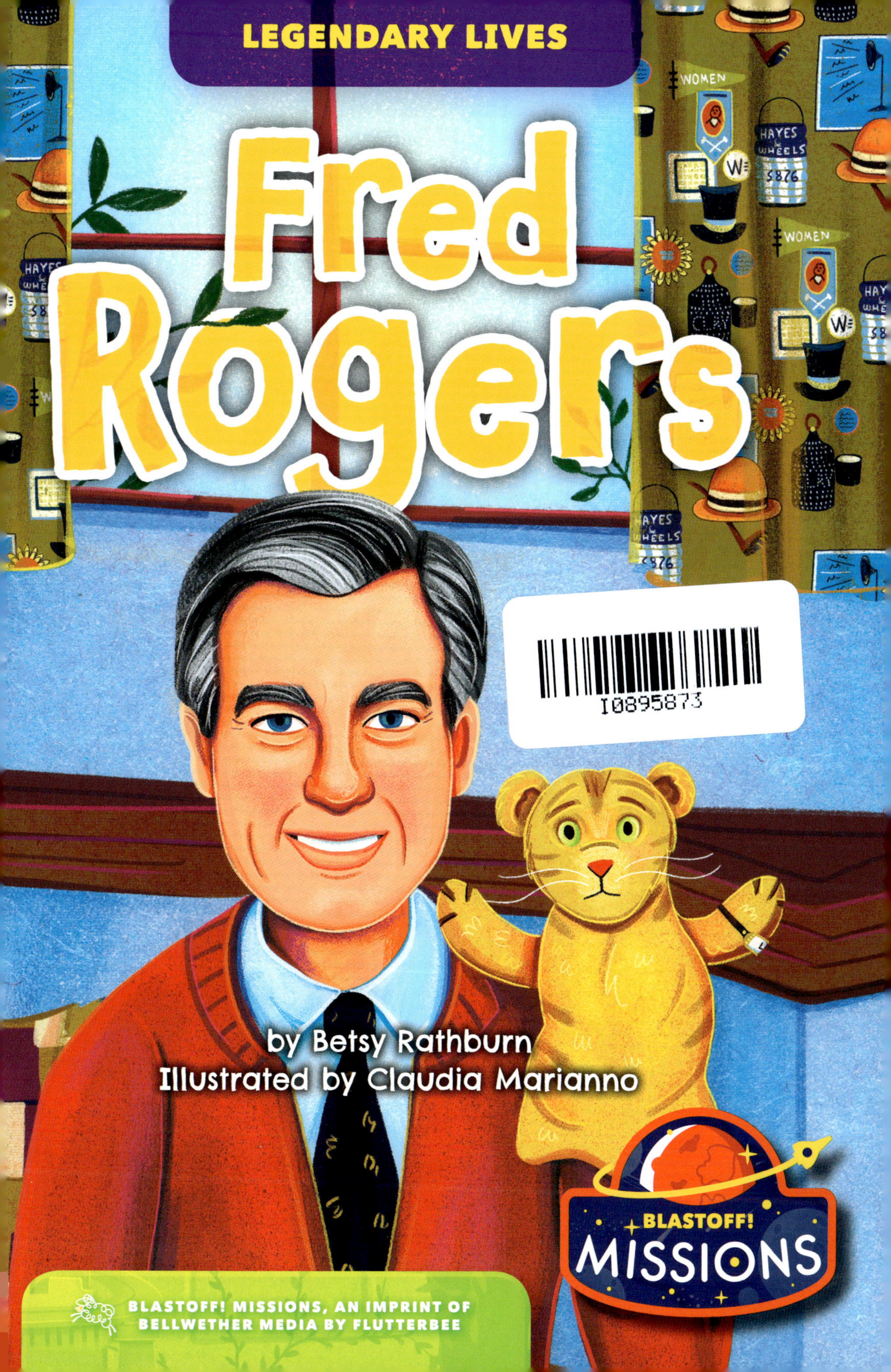

by Betsy Rathburn

Illustrated by Claudia Marianno

BLASTOFF! MISSIONS

BLASTOFF! MISSIONS, AN IMPRINT OF BELLWETHER MEDIA BY FLUTTERBEE

Blastoff! Missions takes you on a learning adventure! Colorful illustrations and exciting narratives highlight cool facts about our world and beyond. Read the mission goals and follow the narrative to gain knowledge, build reading skills, and have fun!

Traditional Nonfiction

Narrative Nonfiction

Blastoff! Universe

MISSION GOALS

- FIND YOUR SIGHT WORDS IN THE BOOK.
- LEARN ABOUT FRED ROGERS'S LIFE.
- LEARN HOW FRED ROGERS BECAME A TELEVISION HOST.

This edition first published in 2026 by Bellwether Media, Inc.

For information regarding permission, write to Bellwether Media, Inc., Attention: Permissions Department, 3500 American Blvd W, Suite 150, Bloomington, MN 55431.

Library of Congress Cataloging-in-Publication Data is available at www.loc.gov or upon request from the publisher.

ISBN: 9798893048445 (hardcover)
ISBN: 9798898800185 (paperback)
ISBN: 9798893049442 (ebook)

Editor: Rebecca Sabelko Designer: Andrea Schneider

Printed in the United States of America, North Mankato, MN.

This is **Blastoff Jimmy**! He is here to help you on your mission and share fun facts along the way!

Table of Contents

A Beautiful Day

Fred Rogers puts on his sweater. He changes his shoes. It is time for *Mister Rogers' Neighborhood.*

Today, he shares a crayon **factory** with viewers. It is a beautiful day in the neighborhood!

Learning to Explore

Fred is a lonely child. He is sick a lot. He stays home.

He likes to play puppets. He uses his **imagination**.

Today, Fred visits his grandpa. His grandpa **encourages** him.

He teaches Fred new things. He lets Fred **explore**. He helps Fred feel good about himself.

JIMMY SAYS
The Mr. McFeely character from Mister Rogers' Neighborhood was based on Fred's grandpa.

On Television

Fred has finished **college**. He now works for a **public television** station. He makes music and puppets for *The Children's Corner*.

Daniel Tiger is one of Fred's puppets. He lives in a clock!

The Children's Corner

JIMMY SAYS

Daniel Tiger is still popular! Many kids like *Daniel Tiger's Neighborhood.*

It is 1968. Fred has his own show now. *Mister Rogers' Neighborhood* includes many characters he created.

JIMMY SAYS

Fred's show started in Canada. His first appearance on television was on a show called *Misterogers*.

Mister Rogers' Neighborhood

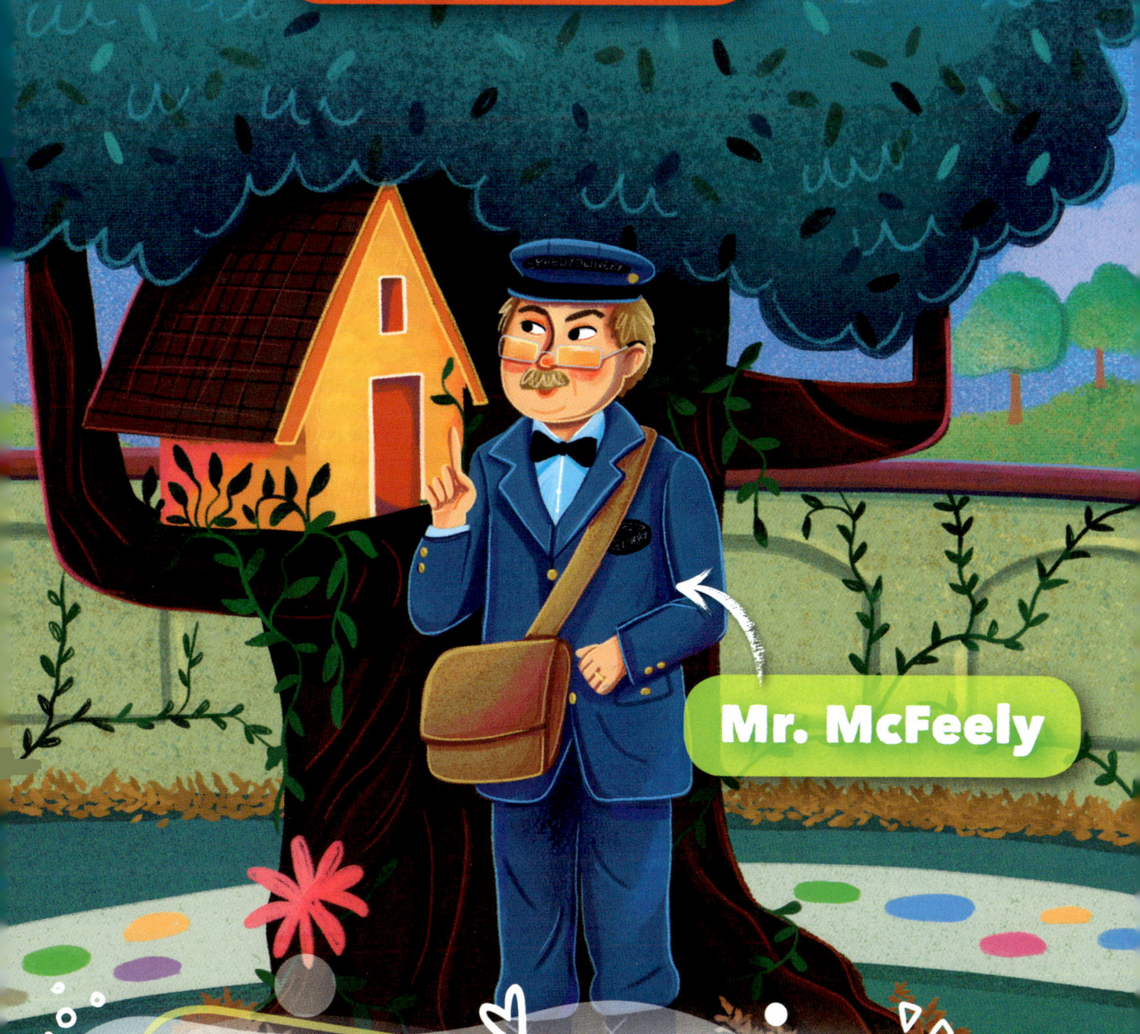

King Friday rules the Neighborhood of Make-Believe. Mr. McFeely brings mail!

Fred speaks in front of the **Senate**. The government wants to cut **funding** for public television.

Fred explains how important public television is for kids. The government decides not to cut funding!

Fred's show has become well-known for helping kids learn about their feelings.

Today, Fred talks about anger. He sings "What Do You Do with the Mad That You Feel?"

I like you just the way you are.

The last episode of *Mister Rogers' Neighborhood* has aired on television.

Fred speaks directly to his viewers. He encourages them to be kind to others.

Everyone's Neighbor

Fred is being honored today. He receives the Presidential Medal of Freedom.

People of all ages love his work. They are proud to be his neighbors!

Fred Rogers Profile

Born

March 20, 1928, in Latrobe, Pennsylvania

Died

February 27, 2003

Accomplishments

Created and hosted *Mister Rogers' Neighborhood* from 1968 to 2001

Timeline

1954: starts working on *The Children's Corner*

1968: *Mister Rogers' Neighborhood* begins airing nationwide in the United States

1969: speaks to the Senate about funding for public television

2001: the last episode of *Mister Rogers' Neighborhood* airs

2002: receives the Presidential Medal of Freedom

Glossary

college–a school for higher learning

encourages–gives the help needed to carry out a goal

explore–to travel through a place in order to learn more about it or find something

factory–a building where products are made

funding–money given for a specific purpose

imagination–creative ability

public television–television that is made to educate or entertain others for free and not to earn money; public television needs money from the government to make shows.

Senate–part of the United States government that makes laws

To Learn More

AT THE LIBRARY

Cangelosi, Donna M. *Mister Rogers' Gift of Music.* Salem, Mass.: Page Street Kids, 2022.

Meltzer, Brad. *I Am Mister Rogers.* New York, N.Y.: Rocky Pond Books, 2023.

Rogers, Fred. *A Beautiful Day in the Neighborhood: The Poetry of Fred Rogers.* Philadelphia, Pa.: Quirk Books, 2019.

ON THE WEB

FACTSURFER

Factsurfer.com gives you a safe, fun way to find more information.

1. Go to www.factsurfer.com.

2. Enter "Fred Rogers" into the search box and click 🔍.

3. Select your book cover to see a list of related content.

BEYOND THE MISSION

> WHAT FACT FROM THE BOOK DID YOU THINK WAS THE MOST INTERESTING?

> WHAT QUESTIONS WOULD YOU HAVE ASKED FRED ABOUT HIS LIFE?

> WHAT MAKES YOU FEEL GOOD ABOUT YOURSELF?

Index